D1049963

i am
unicorn
how to embrace your inner power

"Well, now that we have seen each other,"

said the unicorn,

"if you'll believe in me, I'll believe in you."

Lewis Carroll (1832–1898), *Through the Looking-Glass, and What Alice Found There*

i am
unicorn
how to embrace your inner power

kirsten riddle

CICO BOOKS
LONDON NEW YORK

Published in 2018 by CICO Books
An imprint of Ryland Peters & Small Ltd
20–21 Jockey's Fields   341 E 116th St
London WC1R 4BW   New York, NY 10029

www.rylandpeters.com

10 9 8 7 6 5 4 3 2 1

A CIP catalog record for this book is
available from the Library of Congress
and the British Library.

ISBN: 978 1 78249 565 9

Printed in China

Editor: Marion Paull
Designer: Emily Breen
Illustrator: Trina Dalziel

In-house editor: Anna Galkina
Art director: Sally Powell
Production controller: Mai-Ling Collyer
Publishing manager: Penny Craig
Publisher: Cindy Richards

contents

introduction

My love of unicorns began when I was a child.
I adored fantasy stories. I was enthralled by the
epic twists and turns, and pored over reams of fairy tales
to get my fix, but even more than this, I loved storytelling.
I enjoyed making up tales and creating my own imaginary
realm where anything could happen. Some might say that
being an only child fostered this side of my nature. I would
often make my own amusement, but I never felt alone
because I had my imaginary friend Dapple at my side. A
patchwork of colors, with a soft luscious mane and swarthy
tail, Dapple was no ordinary horse. He was a unicorn. His
horn shimmered in the sunlight and when he galloped it was with
such speed and grace, he almost flew. Of course, I knew at
the time that Dapple was a figment of my imagination, but
he seemed real to me and the adventures we went on would
stay with me well into adulthood.

I realize now that Dapple and everything he represented
helped me to tune in to a higher plane and engage my
creative spirit. The unicorn energy that lived within my
imaginary friend helped to fill my life with light and love. It
also stretched my fledgling imagination, sowing the seeds
of my future, even if I didn't know it at the time.

Today I see unicorns from several different points of view.

As a spectator, I enjoy looking at their ethereal beauty, whether in great works of art, illustrations, or on the big screen. There's something about the way they look and move that captures the eye and the heart. It could be argued that a unicorn is simply a horse with a horn protruding from its forehead, but take a second look and you'll see something more. It's as if the light these creatures carry inside seeps from their skin, drawing you in.

As a fan of folklore, I consider how the Ancients around the world saw them. Where did this idea of a horned horse come from, and what did it represent? How has this image evolved over the years, and why does it still fascinate us so much? To me, our ancestors were a wise bunch. They lived with the land, rather than on it. They looked to nature for the answers, and invented narratives to explain some of the biggest mysteries of the earth. The unicorn was an important symbol to them, something they believed in, and it has stood the test of time. We instantly recognize the truth beyond the myth, that this creature is the essence of purity and a symbol of hope to all.

My interest in magic and in folklore go hand in hand, and over the years I've explored many different spiritual practises to find my own path. I've discovered how to work with sacred symbols and mythical creatures, whether that's in the lessons that can be learned from understanding their stories, or in something much deeper—a conjuring up of the energy that would surely resonate from them in the flesh. Unicorns are easy to work with. They're a delight to explore, as you'll discover leafing through the pages of this book. Their influence is everywhere, from high fashion and beauty to the food we prepare. We can bring a touch of unicorn magic to any part of our world, and this book shows you how.

From their origins in history and legend to more mystical associations and how to work some unicorn magic for yourself, each part of the book gives you the lowdown on what you need to know. Up for a bit of unicorn spotting? Never fear, there's the perfect guide to get you started in Part 2, which includes where to look, what to look for, and what to take with you. If you prefer a bit of armchair spotting, relax and peruse the stories and myths at your leisure.

Perhaps you want to tap into unicorn healing energy? That's possible with the techniques I've outlined, showing you how to heal yourself and transmit this energy to others.

If you're a little less concerned with the spiritual and more interested in the practical, there's something for you, too, in Part 3: Unicorn Beauty & Style. Yes, it really is possible to be more unicorn just by revamping your make-up or trying the latest hairstyle. Finally, lest you should be feeling hungry after all your hard work, there's a section of unicorn recipes. This includes setting yourself up for a magical day ahead with a round of unicorn toast, the prettiest breakfast ever! If you're a cake lover, you can try some of the wonderful sweet treats suggested. They may be naughty, but they're also nice and packed full of unicorn goodness. What's not to love?

This book is a treasure trove of unicorn facts and folklore, with a sprinkling of magic on every page. Whatever you're looking for, you should find it here. So let's get started. The unicorns are ready and waiting. They want to invite you into their enchanting world. I guarantee that once you've spent just a little time with these wondrous beasts, you'll never look back.

PART 1

The Magic of
UNICORNS

so what exactly is a unicorn?

Most commonly described as a
mythical beast that takes the
shape of a white horse, it has
a single horn protruding from its

forehead. The name "unicorn" reveals this creature's most
important and unique feature—when translated from Latin,
"unis" means one, and "cornu" means horn. Other than that,
early descriptions vary. Some suggest the creature is more
squat than elegant, with a white body and purple or red
head. The horn also changes. It can be multicolored with
a red tip and white base, and sometimes it's black in the
middle, although this may well allude to the Indian rhinoceros
rather than a unicorn. In some tales the unicorn is deer like,
and in others it resembles a lion with a horn, which is
interesting because according to one long-held belief lions
and unicorns don't get on. It has also been compared to a
statuesque goat, which, along with the other descriptions,
adds to the confusion about what this creature really is.

Classically, the unicorn is pictured as an exquisite, horse-
like mammal, with lithe limbs and a beautiful flowing mane.
Its coat is the purest white, possibly with a silvery tinge. Its
hooves are sturdy like those of a goat, giving it power and
strength. Fantasy and fiction have played a part in changing

this image over the years—variations include a purple or golden coat, and a lion's tail—but while the image is important, what it represents is even more significant. The unicorn has always been a symbol of hope and freedom, a bringer of harmony in all things. Sightings of the creature are rare, and those who have seen it are truly blessed and consider it a sign of good things to come.

Although it's generally agreed that the unicorn is a positive symbol, the meaning of its appearance does vary depending on the part of the world you come from. In China, it's a good omen, and considered sacred. In Scotland, the unicorn takes on even more meaning. It was adopted as the country's national animal by King Robert in the 1300s, most likely because of its outstanding reputation for goodness, and also because it was considered a symbol of protection.

Pure of heart and overflowing with divine power, the unicorn fascinates and intrigues in equal measure, figuring in magic and mythology throughout the ages.

how to harness unicorn power in everyday life

Let's face it, who wouldn't want their own fairy godmother or superhero on call 24/7? Imagine having a supernatural being with amazing powers to back you up in everything you do—and, better still, this assistance comes from a loving source that only ever has your best interests at heart. It's possible to have all this and more in the spectacular shape of the unicorn. Whether you think it's a creature of myth or something more tangible, you can work with its power to manifest the things you want and need. It doesn't matter if you're slightly skeptical, the magic still works. This is because the image of the unicorn is such a potent one it triggers something in the subconscious mind, which in turn makes us respond in the way we think and act. We instantly recognize what the unicorn represents, and the more we focus on it, the more we bring those qualities into our world.

Harnessing the energy of this generous being is easy. If you like, you can perform intricate rituals or spells, and there are some examples in this book to get you started, but you don't have to. It's not essential for the magic to work. Simply incorporating the image of the unicorn into your life is enough to get things moving. You can do this in a number of ways.

* **Fill your house with images of the unicorn:** If you don't want to be full on, just position a couple of small images where you can see them every day and that will make a difference. For those who want to immerse themselves in loving energy, take this a step further and create your own unicorn altar (page 27). Fill it with images and items associated with this creature and use it as a space where you can meditate, find peace, and relax.

* **Go mobile:** Keep an image of a unicorn in your purse or wallet so that you always have it, should the need arise. Also, consider having the image as a screensaver on your computer or phone.

* **Read up on these magical creatures:** Get lost in their world and recreate some of the myths in your mind. Share the tales with those close to you, and try to picture the narratives because this will help you connect to their energy. You could even have a go at creating a unicorn tale of your own, or, if you prefer, a poem or picture. Unicorn magic helps us tap into our creative side.

THINK

LIKE A

UNICORN

* **Strange as it sounds, it's easy to think like a unicorn:** Challenge yourself to exude loving energy at all times. Imagine you're a magical being made up of thousands of particles of light. Every person you encounter picks up on your energy, so be kind and positive. Illuminate someone's world with a smile or a compliment. Small kindnesses lift your energy vibrations and help you connect to the power of the unicorn.

* **Have fun:** Unicorns are playful beings. Their spirits are as light as a feather. You can be the same by simply letting your hair down and doing something you love. Make time for play every day, and do something that makes you happy just for the sake of it.

* **Step outside of your comfort zone:** Challenge yourself to do something adventurous. It might be scary at first, but once you've done it you'll feel a breath of fresh air wash over you. This rush of excitement raises your energy vibration and puts you a step closer to the magical realm where unicorns reside.

channeling unicorn magic

Unicorn magic is deeply powerful stuff. The grace and purity of these beautiful beings brings harmony to every area of life and their loving energy can overcome the biggest hurdle and heal any hurt. To harness this energy, you must allow yourself to become a vessel to the light. Open yourself up and let their magic flow through you!

WHAT TO DO

Massage a few drops of frankincense essential oil into the wax of a white candle to anoint it with cleansing power. This also lifts the energy vibrations and helps you tap into your higher self, the intuitive side of the brain. Light the candle and sit on the floor with your back against the wall for support. Relax your shoulders and keep your spine straight. Close your eyes and breathe deeply for a few minutes.

In your mind, see yourself sitting in a beautiful meadow filled with flowers. The sun is shining and you are bathed in its warmth. The air before you begins to blur and slowly the white figure of a unicorn emerges. It stands before you, gazing lovingly into your eyes. You instantly feel a connection. Gently, the unicorn lowers its head and fires a sphere of golden light from its horn into your heart. This light floods your entire body with joy and washes away any negative energy.

LET THE

MAGIC

BECOME A PART OF

YOU

You may feel a range of emotions, and even experience visions or hear the unicorn speaking to you. Go with the flow and when you're ready, give thanks to the unicorn for blessing you with its magic and say goodbye. Breathe deeply, open your eyes, and give your body a shake to awaken your senses.

Keep a journal of your channeling sessions and make a note of anything you see, feel, or hear. It might not make sense at first, but these psychic messages could become important in the future.

how to tune into the healing power of unicorns

Unicorns are famous for their amazing healing power, which mainly resides in the horn; this is also what makes them vulnerable. Throughout the ages unicorns have been tirelessly hunted for this treasure. Kings, princes, and all manner of noblemen have sought to own one. The horn itself, known as the alicorn, can cure any disease, but what makes it even more desirable is its ability to dispel poison. Folklore tales abound with these majestic beasts saving the day by cleansing poisoned water or other liquids. Goblets made from unicorn horn were prized by those in power who constantly feared betrayal at the hands of someone close. To them, the unicorn horn was a must to protect them from such treachery.

In the Middle Ages, unicorn horns were said to have the power to cure the plague, heal bites from feral animals, and cool a fever, and drinking from the horn was thought to cure epilepsy. But unicorn horns were strictly in the domain of the rich since they were reputedly worth thousands of pounds. It was unlikely that the poor would even catch sight of one.

Mary, Queen of Scots, allegedly had a piece of unicorn horn, which she brought with her from France when she came to claim her throne. A staunch believer in its magical properties, she would dip the broken fragment in her food to test it before eating, so any poison would be ineffective. Even Nicholas Culpeper, the much respected and world-famous botanist and physician, acknowledged the power of the horn. In 1694, he wrote: "Uni-corns horn resists Poyson and the Pestilence, provokes Urine, restores lost strength, brings forth both Birth and Afterbirth."

Many have disputed the existence of real unicorns, claiming the horns in question belonged to other creatures, such as the onager, a wild ass found in Arabia, or the equally unusual pirassoupi, a two-horned hairy creature the size of a mule, which is found near the Red Sea. If not these animals, then the horns could have come from a rhinoceros or narwhal. Whatever the truth may be, unicorns are a universal symbol of hope and healing. Their energy can be used to heal, provide comfort, and cleanse body, mind, and soul.

unicorns lift our

hearts

UNICORN HEALING RITUAL

There are many ways to tap into the healing power of unicorns. This simple ritual will help you get started. The key is to do what feels right for you. Working with unicorn energy is a personal thing, and you'll instinctively know the best way to connect to this power.

Start by creating the right atmosphere for healing work. To cleanse the area and encourage the flow of positive energy, burn frankincense essential oil, or add a couple of drops to a small bowl of warm water and let the fragrance fill the room. Somewhere central, in your line of vision, light a tall white candle to represent the unicorn's healing horn. Sit comfortably, with your shoulders relaxed and your hands resting palm upward in receiving position.

Begin by focusing on the candle in front of you. Gaze at the flame and imagine it getting taller. You may notice the flame seems to stretch as if it's influenced by your thoughts. See it getting brighter and watch how it flickers and bends in a dance with the air. Close your eyes and imagine the flame sitting behind your eyes. It extends upward and flows out of the top of your head, connecting you to the spirit realm. Now picture yourself sitting in the center of four unicorns. Each one represents an element—earth, air, fire, and water. The unicorns send threads of blue healing light from

For a quick energy boost
anytime, anywhere,
picture a unicorn sending
healing light from its horn
directly to your heart. Choose a color that
matches the type of energy you need:

Red	action, assertiveness, passion
Blue	general healing, strength
Gold	confidence, charm
White	cleansing, purification
Purple	intuition, personal power
Green	inspiration, growth
Pink	loving energy, compassion
Amber	grounding, balance

their horns in your direction. Each strand connects with
the flame above your head, making it bigger and brighter.
When you're ready, imagine the flame being absorbed back
through your head into your body. Feel it burning strong,
flooding every cell of your body with healing light. Breathe
deeply and enjoy the sensation of peace and strength.

SEND UNICORN HEALING ENERGY TO OTHERS

Before you begin, find a picture of the person to whom you'd like to send help, either an actual photograph or one on your phone. If you prefer, you can write the name on a piece of paper. As long as you're holding, in both hands, something that connects you to this person, it doesn't matter what it is. Perform the usual healing ritual. Then, as you visualize the flame being absorbed back into your body, imagine the light and heat pouring from your hands into whatever it is you're holding. Picture the person in your mind, and see them happy and healed. Finish by thanking the unicorns for their assistance.

To maintain a steady flow of healing energy to someone who is suffering from an ongoing condition, take the picture or personal object you've been working with and place it either beneath or next to an image of a unicorn.

creating a unicorn altar

One of the best ways to work with unicorn magic is to create an altar. This doesn't have to be elaborate in design or structure; something simple, such as a coffee table, bookshelf, or windowsill, serves the purpose and makes an excellent starting point. Your altar will act as a focal point and a space where you can perform prayers, spells, and meditations.

To begin, clear away any clutter and cleanse the area by taking a small bowl of hot water and adding either a handful of fresh sage leaves, or a couple of drops of sage essential oil. This uplifting herb is often used in rituals for cleansing and purification. Gently waft the aroma from the bowl around the space, or simply leave it there overnight.

Once the altar is cleansed you can begin to decorate it. Remember, this is your special space to help you connect with unicorn energy. Include, if you can, images of unicorns, and any sculptures or ornaments that you like. Books and texts can be stored on your altar for ease of reference, and if you have a unicorn journal you may want to keep it to hand. A white or silver candle to be lit during spells and meditations will help you raise magical energy. Stones and essential oils can be added, depending on your preference, and glitter, fairy lights, and anything with sparkle will also attract unicorn energy.

To keep the energy moving, update your altar every so often with new images, candles, and stones. You might want to have a unicorn wish box where you can store any wishes, mantras, or spells. Again, this doesn't have to be ornate. A small gift box that you like will do the trick, and you can decorate it to your taste.

DECORATION GUIDE

Unicorn colors

White
Silver
Pink
Violet
Purple
Gold
Light green
Light blue
Turquoise

Unicorn stones

Moonstone
Rose quartz
Quartz
Aquamarine
Citrine
Peridot
Turquoise
Amethyst

Unicorn scents

Rose
Frankincense
Geranium
Lavender

Jasmine
Sandalwood
Orange
Ylang ylang

unicorn spells

Unicorns represent love, innocence, and purity. They bring clarity, light, and healing to any situation and can help you open your heart, find inspiration, and unleash your creative spirit. There are many different unicorn spells. Some focus on connecting with unicorn energy; others utilize symbols and use specific ingredients to summon unicorn magic.

There is no right or wrong way to perform a unicorn spell. The only necessity is that everything is done with a loving heart and a positive intention. Unicorn magic cannot be used to control or manipulate another, or cause harm in any way.

You can adapt spells to suit, using some of the ingredients suggested, or create your own rituals. The key, as with all magic, is to be flexible and make it personal so that it fits with your aim.

To help you get started, here are some of the most effective unicorn spells.

A SPELL TO HEAL A BROKEN HEART

Often hailed as the Guardian of the Sea, the unicorn has a reputation for healing hearts and washing away pain of any kind. This spell works with the element of water and salt to soothe a broken heart.

What to do

Take a small, square, white handkerchief or piece of material. In the center place a pinch of dried vervain, a herb associated with matters of the heart. Join the corners of the material together and tie with string or ribbon. If possible, soak the bundle in a little sea water. If not, take a small bowl of fresh water and mix in a teaspoon of sea salt; then dip the bundle in the bowl. Squeeze away the excess water and say, "Guardian of the Sea, soothe this tender heart. With every drop of water, I seek a new start. Heal the hurt that binds me, set my soul free. With your loving power, sweet Guardian of the Sea." When you've finished, let the bundle dry in the sunshine. Keep it about your person for a week. During this time, you should start to feel more positive and less hurt.

A SPELL TO FIND LOVE

Unicorns love flowers. Sweet scent and vibrant colors draw them close. It's common to see pictures of unicorns surrounded by flowers, standing in wildflower meadows, or adorned with blooms. This spell uses their connection to flowers to help you attract romance.

What to do

You'll need some pink and red roses, or carnations. Place them in a vase in front of you and close your eyes. Spend some time quietly connecting to your unicorn guide. Picture it standing before you. Around its neck you notice a garland of pink and red flowers. This garland is the unicorn's gift to you. Picture yourself holding the flowers in both hands. As you do this, you're bathed in a pink glow. You feel safe and loved. Next, imagine the type of partner you'd like to attract. If you can picture him or her in your mind, see yourself in a warm embrace, blissfully happy. Say, "It is as I see. What I picture is for me." Open your eyes and spend a few minutes gazing at the flowers. Every day when you refresh the water, repeat the magical chant and imagine you're bathed in pink light.

A SPELL FOR GUIDANCE

The eyes of a unicorn hold many truths. Wise and loving, these beings come from a higher plane and instinctively know how to help you. If you're looking for guidance in any area of life, this simple spell will help to open your eyes to the innate well of knowledge within.

What to do

Find an image of a unicorn in which you can clearly see its beautiful, expressive eyes. Spend a few minutes gazing at the picture, paying attention to the eyes. When you're ready, close your eyes and focus on your breathing. Take long breaths in and out until you feel totally relaxed. Now imagine you're looking into the eyes of a unicorn. See them growing in size, getting larger and larger until you can almost step into them. Feel yourself drawn into the inky darkness. Imagine stepping inside those eyes and feel the wisdom within envelop you. Know that you now have all the answers you need in your own life. You have been given the gift of great knowledge. If any thoughts come to you at this time, be sure to write them down. They may be insights that can help you in the future.

A SPELL FOR SUCCESS

Rainbows are often associated with unicorns. Some stories even suggest that their horn can produce a rainbow of healing light. In folklore, rainbows are considered a lucky symbol. They bring hope, success, and abundance. This ritual uses the power of the rainbow combined with unicorn energy to help you achieve any goal.

What to do

Draw a large rainbow on a piece of paper. Have fun with this and spend some time coloring it in and decorating the page. Beneath the arch of the rainbow, write a few words to sum up the kind of success you'd like, for example: "I get the recognition I deserve at work and a pay rise," or "I get my dream house/trip/man." Put the paper in an envelope and place it beneath a picture or model of a unicorn. Say, "Bless me with your magic, make my dream come true."

A SPELL TO ENCOURAGE PROPHETIC VISIONS AND DREAMS

Moonstone is often associated with unicorns because of the unicorn's connection with the moon and water. This stone balances the emotions while improving intuitive skills. It can be used in conjunction with unicorn energy to stimulate psychic abilities and help you see into the future.

What to do

Before bed, spend a
few minutes clearing your
mind of clutter. Breathe
deeply and imagine you're gazing at the moon. Feel yourself
showered in its illuminating light. Close your eyes and press the
moonstone against the middle of your forehead. This is where
the third eye energy center is located. Imagine a ball of white
light extending outward from this area. It stretches to form a
horn with a point, not unlike a unicorn horn. This beam of light
connects you to the universe and helps you receive any
psychic messages or visions. When you're ready, open your
eyes and place the moonstone beneath your pillow to
encourage prophetic dreams.

A SPELL FOR CREATIVITY

White feathers are often associated with unicorns, and some believe that finding a feather, particularly somewhere unexpected, can mean you've been visited by one of these glorious beasts. Feathers are linked to the element of air, which represents thoughts and ideas. Working with this element fires the imagination and allows you to engage with your creative spirit.

What to do

Add a couple of drops of bergamot essential oil to a small bowl of warm water. This uplifting scent promotes creativity. As the steam rises from the bowl, take a white feather and begin to waft the aroma around your head. Breathe deeply as you do so and enjoy the lovely fragrance. Do this for a couple of minutes until you feel totally immersed in the scent. Hold the feather in both hands, close your eyes, and picture yourself in the presence of a unicorn. Call upon its power to help you express yourself creatively.

A SPELL FOR PERSONAL POWER

Quartz is another crystal associated with unicorns. It has the power to transmit and amplify energy, which makes it ideal when you need a boost. Those who work with unicorn energy often see these creatures emerging from a crystal cavern or with quartz crystal horns.

What to do

Invest in a quartz crystal point and spend some time charging it with positive energy. The easiest way to do this is to breathe positivity into the crystal. Take a deep breath in and as you breathe out imagine you're pouring rays of sunlight into every facet. Next, take a bowl of warm water and add two or three drops of lavender essential oil. Dip the crystal into the bowl and sprinkle drops of water over your head and the rest of your body. Every drop that falls is cleansing your aura, the energy field around your body, making it shine brighter than ever. When you've finished, hold the crystal in both hands, breathe deeply, and imagine drawing the positive energy into your heart.

FRIENDSHIP and UNICORN MAGIC go hand in hand

A SPELL TO MAKE NEW FRIENDS

Anything that brings laughter and love into our lives attracts unicorns. They adore joyful atmospheres, and enjoy seeing us engage our playful spirit. These spiritual beings want us to make connections with others and sow the seeds of companionship and compassion.

What to do

Take a handful of wild flower seeds and a bottle of water and venture out into the countryside. Find a quiet secluded spot that looks like it could do with some loving attention. Hold the seeds loosely in your hands and spin around in a circle, letting them fall to the ground. Continue to twirl and say, "The seeds of friendship I do sow, blessed with love they're sure to grow. Unicorn magic I draw near, to help me make new friendships dear." Sprinkle the area with the water and repeat the magical chant.

A SPELL FOR PROTECTION

Unicorns may be full of the light of love but don't let that fool you; they're still incredibly powerful allies and provide potent spiritual protection when required. This spell creates a unicorn shield to keep harmful influences at bay.

What to do

Mark out a circle using stones and stand in the center. Imagine that each stone represents a unicorn. Breathe deeply and draw on the magical energy emanating from these beings. As you do this, picture a thread of light extending from each unicorn to form a dome of light that meets above your head. You are completely sheltered and protected from any kind of negative energy. When you're feeling vulnerable, see the dome of light in your mind and know that the unicorns are keeping you safe from harm.

A SPELL FOR GOOD FORTUNE

The unicorn horn was prized for its healing powers, but it isn't the only horn with mystical associations. The Horn of Plenty, otherwise known as the Cornucopia, had the power to produce an abundance of food and riches. Always overflowing with goodies, the Cornucopia is a symbol of good fortune. Combine this with some unicorn magic and you can turn your luck around.

What to do

While you might not have access to a horn of plenty, you can create something similar in your own home. Find an ornate fruit bowl and place it in a prominent position where everyone can see it, and fill it with colorful bounty. Consider what good fortune means to you. Perhaps it means you'll always have money in your pocket, or food on the table, in which case you might fill the bowl with gold and silver coins, fresh fruit, nuts, and candies. If you want to increase your luck, you might add in some lucky symbols, such as a horseshoe or a key. Think of any personal requests that you have. For example, you might want more love in your life, or a new job. Write all your wishes on pieces of paper and add them to the bowl. This is your magical horn of plenty and it will help you attract the things you need. To finish, place a picture of a unicorn beneath the bowl to give the horn extra power. Every time you remove something from the horn, such as a food item or some coins, try to replace it with something else in order to keep the positive energy flowing.

FIVE QUICK FIXES

Here are some unicorn rituals for when you need a burst of magic to brighten your day and you're short on time!

* **For an instant pick-me-up** imagine a rainbow above your head. It gleams brightly, surrounding you with rays of positive energy.

* **Feeling vulnerable?** Whatever the situation, imagine a unicorn walking by your side. Its warmth and strength are an anchor keeping you safe and secure.

* **Need a psychic insight fast?** Picture a unicorn horn in the center of your forehead. Your third eye chakra, which is associated with psychic skills and intuition, is located in this area. Feel the horn extending outward like an antenna picking up signals and messages from the universe.

* **To feel more loving and attract love** imagine that every time you breathe in, you take in rosy pink energy and every time you breathe out, you shower pretty colored flowers everywhere.

* **Aiming for success?** Whatever the goal or challenge, spend a few minutes every day visualizing yourself on the back of a unicorn. Together you're racing toward the finish line, gliding on air as you reach your target.

unicorn mantras

One of the best ways to bring a little unicorn magic into your life is by using mantras. These positive statements, which include a selection of carefully chosen "power" words, help to reinforce your connection. They focus the mind, so that you can see and feel unicorn energy at work in every experience.

WRITE YOUR OWN

Create your own mantras by putting together some positive statements. Start by setting the right atmosphere to focus your mind. Light a candle and burn some sweet-scented oil. Take a deep breath and set your intention by stating your desire, either out loud or in your head. Say something like, "I wish to create a set of magical mantras to help me move forward in every area of my life." Then ask the unicorns to guide you.

Think about the kind of qualities you'd like to bring to your life, and the areas where you need help, and then compose your statement. For example, if you'd like to have more fun and bring a little lightness into your world, you might say, "The unicorn within helps me bring out my playful side."

As a guide to get you started, here are some uplifting unicorn mantras. Choose one or two and repeat them several times every day for a couple of weeks to see positive changes manifest.

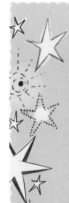

Place your mantra where you'll see it every day. For example, write it on a post-it note and stick it to your mirror, computer, bulletin board, or fridge. Every time you see it, make a point of reading it through.

To give your mantra added oomph, conjure up an image of a unicorn in your mind. See it radiating loving white light. Imagine you are bathed in this light as you repeat the mantra.

I AM
STRONG
I AM
BEAUTIFUL
I AM
UNICORN!

LET THE LIGHT OF THE

UNICORN

ILLUMINATE YOUR PATH
EVERY DAY

THINK

LOVE

THINK

UNICORN

wherever I go,
I walk with

unicorns

I look at the

world

through the eyes of a

unicorn

WHEN LIFE DRAGS
YOU DOWN, THE
UNICORN
LIFTS
YOU UP

RUN
FREE

BE

UNICORN

unicorn magic

flows through me

I believe in

unicorns

because they

believe in

me

BE HAPPY

YOUR

unicorn

LOVES YOU

I EMBODY UNICORN MAGIC

the

loving

energy of the

unicorn

radiates through me

WHEN TIMES ARE
DARK,
LET THE
UNICORN
BE YOUR
LIGHT

A
smile,
is a
unicorn kiss

PART 2

UNICORN
Spotting

myth and legend

Captivating and timeless, the legend of the unicorn has existed in folklore for centuries. It may be a mythical creature, but the unicorn has a special relationship with humankind and features prominently in literature and art. Its luminescent skin tone, ethereal mane, and saber-like horn make it stand out from the crowd, but how it looks is not the only thing that makes it memorable. Its nature is one of innocence and love in its purest form. According to one tale, when the animals piled on Noah's Ark two by two, the unicorn was too busy playing and missed the boat, which is why this enigmatic creature no longer exists here on earth. Or does it?

Some believe that if you're pure of heart and in the right place at the right time, you might catch a glimpse, a quick peek between the veil that separates worlds.

In fiction, virgin maids were thought to attract unicorns, their innocence a beacon to draw it closer. Fairies, too, were thought to protect its magic, and some tales tell of the unicorn existing in a fey otherworld.

Passages in the bible mention a fantastical creature called a re'em, which is both strong and horned. This Hebrew word was later translated into unicorn and in some cases rhinoceros, although its correct meaning is wild ox. A mighty animal, it was deemed fierce and could be caught only if a virgin maid was thrown in its path. Another passage relates the tale of a great fight between a unicorn and an elephant, a battle that ultimately led to the elephant's demise.

One of the earliest sightings of unicorns came from India. The Greek physician and historian Ctesias described its appearance and claimed that its horn, which was prized by Indian princes, had the power to prevent any poisoning. Other reports describe the creature emerging from rivers and lakes and it is often pictured standing by water in works of art. One particular tale speaks of the unicorn rising from the ocean early in the morning and dipping its horn into a poisoned lake to expel the venom so that the other animals could drink from it.

However and whenever this being appears, one thing is certain—you cannot engineer a meeting. It is up to the unicorn to find you, if it chooses. Having said that, there are certain locations where you'll stand more chance of spotting it.

TOP UNICORN SPOTTING SITES

* Secluded rivers, lakes, or streams
* Deserted beaches
* Meadows with fairy rings
  (circles of flowers or mushrooms)
* Mountains and hilltops
* Near waterfalls
  and wells
* Mounds with
  caves or
  crevices

essential equipment

Unicorn spotting is not an exact science, but some items may help you in your search and should be part of your "spotting toolkit."

Binoculars

Unicorns are notoriously hard to see. They move between the realms with super speed and agility, their passage so quick that it can almost appear as a shimmer of light to the naked eye. They are also wary of human contact, so if you are lucky enough to see one, it will still be from a great distance, which is why binoculars are an essential part of your field kit.

Notebook and pen

It's important to keep a record of any sightings, not only for evidence, but to help you discover any patterns and trends. While a unicorn is unlikely to turn up in exactly the same spot twice, it may feel comfortable in certain areas and at specific times, so keeping a note of where and when you saw one will give you an insight into its movements and habits. Pen and paper are also helpful should inspiration strike—the presence of unicorns is often the catalyst for creative endeavors—and to stave off boredom. Unicorn spotting can be a long and arduous task, so be prepared to entertain yourself!

These days, it's almost second nature to have your phone, or some other form of gadgetry, to hand, but unicorns are not impressed by modern technology. They're spiritual beings and they work with energy on a higher plane, so if you really want to spot one or at least connect to their magic, keep devices switched off. They're more likely to approach when they feel that an area is free from electromagnetic waves. Disconnecting will also help you feel more relaxed and open to intuitive messages, visions, and sightings.

Sweet treats

It's always a good idea to have snacks on hand when you're off on your adventures, but even more so if you're hoping to spot a unicorn. These magical creatures adore sweet treats. As well as eating the more traditional diet of hay, oats, and grass, they enjoy a sugary nibble. While it's highly unlikely you'll get that close, you may be able to tempt them nearer with a tasty offering. Opt for things that are homemade (check out the recipes in this book for inspiration) and pretty to look at. Think rainbow pancakes and cookies, unicorn cakes, and multicolored candy sprinkles!

Pillow

You never know where you'll end up on your travels. Unicorns can appear in some strange locations, so it's always a good idea to have a pillow to hand. You may be sitting for some time and it's important to be comfortable. Unicorns are less likely to approach if you're fidgeting, or look ill at ease. They respond to an air of calm, and any erratic movement will scare them away.

Rose water

This alluring scent is particularly attractive to unicorns. They love the smell of roses and are often pictured standing amid these beautiful blooms. Invest in rose-water spray, or make it yourself—soak a large handful of rose petals in warm water, strain, and decant into a bottle. Douse yourself liberally. A unicorn won't be deceived into thinking you're a flower, but it will appreciate the pleasant aroma.

COUNTRIES WHERE YOU'RE MOST LIKELY TO SEE A UNICORN

Scotland
Greece
India
France
China

PLACES WHERE YOU'RE LEAST LIKELY TO SPOT A UNICORN

* **Any city** Unicorns are not fans of built-up areas with lots of noise and people. They prefer peace and solitude and hate pollution of any kind. High-rise buildings, busy streets, and traffic congestion are a no no.

* **In the jungle** These spiritual beings would feel highly uncomfortable surrounded by so many predators.

* **On a popular summer beach** The combination of people and heat would most likely put them off. Also, unicorns have light-colored coats so they must be careful in the sun!

* **On top of a tall building** Although they can cope with heights, being surrounded by concrete would weigh down their energy, leaving them tired and sluggish.

where will i find unicorns in popular culture?

Unicorns are everywhere—literally. They crop up in fiction, poetry, and rhyme. They shine from the big screen and the television screen. They peer from art paper and canvas of every description, whether in acrylic, watercolor, oil, or tapestry threads. These beatific beings seem to leap into our hearts. It doesn't matter where you are in the world, the level of your understanding or knowledge, you cannot fail to come across the unicorn at some point in your life.

FOLKTALES

It's easy to see why unicorns feature in many folktales from around the world. These stories usually illustrate a moral or deliver a salient lesson, and unicorns, being symbols of light and love, make the perfect teachers. They show us the error of our ways. In some cases, they demonstrate a new and more loving way to behave.

In the Tibetan folktale "The Hunter and the Unicorn," a hunter falls down the side of a cliff. As he hangs there by the tips of his fingers, he pleads for help. A unicorn comes to his rescue, pulling the man to safety. Unfortunately, the hunter is a cruel man and instead of sticking to his promise not to harm unicorns represent hope & the human spirit

the unicorn, he kills it. But he doesn't know the road ahead. After walking around in circles for days, the man becomes tired and weak. Half-starved and confused, he once more falls down the cliff. This time there's no one to save him.

The unicorn appears in Winifred Finlay's book of Scottish yarns, *Folk Tales from Moor and Mountain*. In "The fair maid and the snow-white unicorn," a magical tale, the unicorn, a lifelong guardian of the fair maid, turns out to be a prince who is both wise and kind of heart. He demonstrates this in his actions, once again teaching readers that real happiness lies in helping others.

NOVELS AND MOVIES

Not solely limited to folktales, unicorns also make their presence known in novels, stories, and literary works. Lewis Carroll, in his famous children's book *Through the Looking Glass*, includes the rhyme "The lion and the unicorn," which details the two creatures fighting over the crown of the White King. That fight is mentioned again in Neil Gaiman's more contemporary novel *Stardust*. Alan Garner, In his 1965 book *Elidor*, includes a lost unicorn from another world, and a few years later *The Last Unicorn* was born in the form of a novel by Peter S. Beagle, which was turned into a film of the same name in 1982.

More recently, unicorns have featured in the super-popular series of Harry Potter books, and appeared on movie screens in the 2005 adaptation of *The Lion, the Witch, and the Wardrobe*.

It might seem that these creatures dwell only in the realms of fantasy and sweet children's books, but they surface in other, more surprising genres. One made gruesome use of its horn in the 2012 horror film "Cabin in the woods," while another cropped up in "Tropico," songstress Lana del Rey's short film about sin and redemption—proof, if any was needed, that you never know when or where a unicorn will pop up. They are as surprising as they are enigmatic.

HERALDRY

This is one of the best places to spot unicorns. They are a common feature in coats of arms and on family crests. Closely associated with royalty, it's thought that this and the creature's noble reputation are the key reasons for its popularity. Before England and Scotland came under joint rule, Scotland's coat of arms featured two unicorns supporting a shield. One of the earliest examples, carved in the fifteenth century, can be seen at Rothesay Castle on the Isle of Bute. The Celts

believed the unicorn to be a symbol of bravery, intelligence, and joy. No wonder the Scots adopted it as their national animal. It has maintained this status and is now a common symbol associated with the country.

When Scotland and England united, a new coat of arms was created, depicting the Scottish unicorn facing the English lion. This powerful image symbolized the strength of the union between both countries, but in truth the lion and the unicorn were already immortalized in the old nursery rhyme (quoted by Lewis Carroll) that had a less favorable outcome.

The Lion and the Unicorn

The lion and the unicorn
Were fighting for the crown
The lion beat the unicorn
All around the town
Some gave them white bread
And some gave them brown
Some gave them plum cake
And drummed them out of town

unicorn tales

Thousands of unicorn tales may exist already, but why not let this mythic creature inspire you to create your own? Not only is this an excellent way to learn about unicorns, it will also help you tap into their unique energy. As you form a narrative, you'll connect on a spiritual level and begin to understand how they think and feel. This exercise will stretch your imagination and encourage you to develop your artistic side.

Here are a few pointers to help you get started.

* **Look at existing tales for inspiration:** If there's a story you like, have a go at re-working it. Give it a new ending, or create an entirely new tale using the same characters.
* **Create a storyboard:** Working in pictures is an interesting way to build a story and help you tune in to the characters.
* **Consider simple scenarios:** For example, what would happen if you came across a unicorn? Imagine you're a journalist interviewing someone who's had a unicorn experience. What would you want to know? Use your answers as the basis for your tale.

When you feel comfortable and happy with your efforts, try taking the idea of unicorn tales a step further and use stories as a way of receiving guidance from the spirit realms.

TRY THIS

Think of a problem or an area where you need help. Imagine you're telling the story of how you reached this point. Create a short storyboard, using pictures and a sentence or two to describe what's happening in each box. When you reach the point of crisis, the point where the problem or situation has come to a head, introduce your unicorn character. It doesn't matter how unlikely or ridiculous this may feel to the plot; the idea is that you introduce an element of unicorn magic. Use the narrative to ask the unicorn to help you and see where the story leads. Be creative and have fun with this. Looking at a real-life situation as if it's a story can help you see all the options. It's a way of being objective and opening up to other possibilities. Give the story a positive ending and read it through daily to reinforce the idea that whatever happens there will be a satisfactory outcome to your situation.

unicorn myths

Unicorns are steeped in myth and legend. As in many captivating yarns, truth and fiction have blurred over the years so it's hard to tell what came first. Did unicorns spring from fiction, or is there some substance to the tales and could unicorns really exist?

Mentions and sightings come from around the world, but it was first the Ancient Greeks and then the Persians and Romans who suggested that unicorns hailed from India. They saw India as a mysterious and exotic land, a place where all manner of magical creatures lived, so it made sense that unicorns had their home there. Although sightings were reported, it's hard to say whether these were based on fact, or the fanciful musings of an overactive imagination. The fleeting appearance of a goat from a certain angle might give the impression of a creature with one horn and many scholars have suggested that this is the reason ancient carvings and pictures show unicorn-type creatures. This theory could also go some way to explain why unicorns were often depicted with the swarthy legs of the goat. Others who have studied unicorn myths suggest that the creatures could be based on a genetic abnormality. A deer or an ass with one horn instead of two would be highly unusual but it's still a possibility. To those without knowledge of science, it would seem a feat of great magic.

Even now it's hard to disentangle myth from reality, but in truth, does it really matter? Unicorns exist in our imaginations. They have struck a chord with us on many levels, and unlike other mystical creatures, they bring myriad positive traits to the table. They're not monsters created from a specific fear, or to teach a lesson. They're sacred, unique, and lovable— a blessing in animal form. They have lived in our psyche for thousands of years because of this. Unicorns break down the barriers of race, creed, and religion and unite us in one common belief. It doesn't matter who you are, it's hard to resist their attraction. After all, who doesn't want that kind of magic in their life?

UNICORNS
BRING US
TOGETHER

how do i meet my unicorn guide?

Any creature, mythical or otherwise, can be used as a spirit guide and unicorns are no exception. These spiritual beings will provide love and support when called upon. Each person has their own unicorn guide suited to their needs and with a distinct energy that can be tapped into. You can communicate with your guide at any time, and as you get more practiced you'll learn to recognize its voice and any intuitive signs it sends you. To start you'll need to create a sacred meeting place where you can connect with your unicorn guide.

WATER RITUAL

Due to unicorns' strong association with water, it's best if this ritual is carried out when you are bathing. This also creates a relaxing atmosphere, which will enable you to open up your subconscious and communicate on a higher level.

As you dip in the water, take a moment to clear your head. Picture the sea before you and notice the ebb and flow of the waves. Imagine them washing all thoughts and worries from your mind. Take a deep breath and lower yourself further into the water (if you're using a bowl, immerse your feet and imagine you're in the sea). Feel yourself cocooned in warmth. Now imagine you're floating and you can feel a comforting presence in the water with you. This presence is calling to you. Together you are pulled toward the beach and as you emerge you see that you are in the company of a beautiful unicorn.

This is your spirit guide, unique to you. Ask it for a name, and begin to communicate. This is your chance to say what's on your mind, ask for help or a specific message. It may speak in your head, or through your emotions. It will be a different experience for everyone. You may experience a deep sense of calm and a stillness in your heart and mind from the spiritual connection you have formed.

Practice this visualization regularly and you'll find it easy to connect with your unicorn guide at other times.

UNICORN TIPS (FOR KEEN SPOTTERS)

Unicorns speak to us in many ways. You may see a picture of one that leads you to a place where you've never been and a new experience. Be open in heart and mind and you'll soon learn to recognize the signs they send your way.

keep looking

While you may never see one of these stunning creatures in the flesh, you can still do a spot of unicorn hunting by looking for books, magazines, and movies that feature them. When we engage in a narrative, whether a book, a movie, or something we're listening to, we become part of the tale. We connect with the emotions and themes, and immerse ourselves in the energy of the story. It makes sense then that when we indulge in unicorn narratives, we are tapping in to a deep well of magic that resonates with our psyche.

It's a universal rule that like attracts like. When we think positively, we attract positive things and vice versa. The same goes for the things we're interested in. Don't be afraid to share your love of unicorns by wearing unicorn jewelry and clothes, filling your home with unicorn-inspired furnishings and decorations, and even styling your hair/nails/make-up in this way (see Part 3 for ideas). Spread the love and tell others why these creatures are so special!

Unicorns are light, playful beings and they're attracted to these qualities in humans. Be spontaneous and make time for fun. Think like a child and see the wonder in the world around you. The more you practice this way of looking at things, the more likely you are to have a unicorn experience.

A Brief Exchange

As I traversed the vale one morn,

I spied a creature with a horn.

Translucent skin, so pearly white

and statuesque, it was a sight.

In its eyes, a sweet repose

a secret, something no one knows.

The truth of all mankind to bear.

Upon each hoof, the weight lies there.

Yet when it saw me all alone

I heard its voice in fluted tone.

Into my mind it spoke a charm

an ancient magic meant to calm.

And in that very brief exchange

my soul did swiftly re-arrange.

My heart, once broken quickly sealed

And all about me then was healed.

PART 3

UNICORN
Beauty & Style

the spirit of the unicorn

The idea of emulating a magical creature might sound odd but this type of behavior has been practiced throughout history. Many mystical sages and shamans from around the world have copied certain animals, taking on aspects of their appearance to tap in to their power on a spiritual level. They might don furs or wear an antlered headdress to help them tune in. In some cases, they even practiced moving and sounding like the animal in question, again to help them connect.

This kind of worship has been practiced for centuries and is a popular way of celebrating the power of such creatures, mythical and otherwise. In Crete, the Minoan Bee Goddess was revered, and the bee itself was considered sacred. Followers, mostly priestesses, would adorn themselves with giant wings and dance around in a circle, imitating the waggle

dance of the honey bees they lovingly looked after. As unusual as it may sound, this was deeply symbolic and a sign of respect for this winged gem.

While modeling yourself on the mystical unicorn might not be your aim, there's nothing wrong with having a bit of light-hearted fun. It's easy to capture the spirit of the unicorn in the way you look and feel, and it's a great way to revamp your image and give it a magical twist. Think light, airy, and colorful and you are halfway there. A plethora of dazzling cotton-candy shades from head to toe with plenty of sparkle is what this fashion statement entails—My Little Pony meets fairy princess. The unicorn is about playful experimentation and provides a great excuse to try something different, which in turn can bring positive results in every area of your life. So if you want to look great and reap the rewards, read on!

unicorn-colored tresses

There's nothing more beautiful than the flowing mane of a unicorn. It comes in many colors, feels as light as a feather, yet remains strong as steel should you ever need to grasp it in a moment of danger. In pictures, it trickles like a waterfall, all loose curls catching the light. It's a piece of fairy-tale magic and the good news is that you can have your own, with a little adventurous styling.

Hair trends come and go, but unicorn hair is different because you can personalize it to suit your taste and it doesn't have to last long, depending on the dye you choose, which means you can even match it to your outfit! Whether you want a soft raspberry ripple effect, or something more daring, such as blueberry mixed with cherry blossom, you can choose your color mix to create a bold new look. Think pretty pastels and rainbow shades to start with, then accessorize with hair glitter or spray. The dyes used tend to be vegan and semi-permanent, which means they'll gradually fade, giving you an ethereal appearance. It also means it's easy to update the look. The aim is fey, as though you've stepped from the fairy realm with your trusty one-horned steed at your side. If you want to try this look at home, follow these steps and prepare to get messy. Just remember, the unicorn look is so worth it!

Step one

Think of your hair as a blank canvas. To perfect the range of pastel shades and get the right look, you need a plain and balanced backdrop; otherwise the colors won't have the same impact. Start with the lightest blond shade you can get, all over. A silver or ash blond provides a brilliant evenly toned base for your foray into the rainbow world of coloring.

Step two

Separate the locks of hair you'd like to color. Some people want to do the whole head, others prefer to leave a layer of lighter colored hair underneath, which accentuates the overall effect. There's no set way of doing this. If you're unsure, go for a partial look and keep the colors light. Then if you like it, you can be more adventurous next time. If you're looking for perfection, separate each strand with foil, but the easiest thing to do is clip up the hair you don't want to dye to keep it out of the way. The colors will blend and bleed into each other but this is part of the look, and the fun!

Step three

You'll need a mixing bowl, some conditioner (plain white, don't go for colored as this will upset the balance in your dye and affect the final shade), gloves to protect your hands, and a mixing brush, along with your selection of hair dyes. Vegetable dyes are the best option as they won't damage your hair, or the environment. Think multicolored unicorn mane and go for pink, purple, turquoise, and light green shades. Start with the lightest shade, for example pink, and pour it into the bowl. Add three parts conditioner to every one part dye, as this will keep your locks nourished and shiny. Don't worry if the color looks bright in the bowl, it usually comes out lighter and fades rapidly (after a few washes).

Step four

Begin applying the color by taking a strand of hair and working in the dye from the root to the tip. Pin each strand of hair into a small bun to keep it out of the way while you're working on the rest of your head. Once you're happy with the amount of the first color you've applied, wash your hands and the bowl, and repeat the procedure for the next shade and so on, until your entire head has been treated.

Step five

When you're happy that you've colored the right amount of hair with your choice of hues, clip it out of the way, and leave for half an hour before the great color reveal. Rinse your hair thoroughly in warm water and a little shampoo.

Step six

You now have a beautiful rainbow of hair to play with. Style it into loose curls, braid it, tie it up into a high pony tail, the world is your oyster– or unicorn! To give a final magical touch, decorate with stars, flowers, and lots of sparkle.

unicorn-colored tresses 91

unicorn make-up

It's not just hair that's having a unicorn moment. The beauty world has been taken by storm and it's not surprising when you consider the parallels between your make-up bag and this mythical beast. Make-up is a magical tool that helps us look and feel sensational. It has the power to transform with the flick of a wand, albeit one with a brush at the end. Unicorns are the pure essence of magic, a symbol of beauty in all its abundance, so when the two meet, wonderful things happen! Think effervescent cotton-candy colors that look sweet enough to eat, the kind of shimmering shades that will give your skin an almost supernatural luminescence.

This is the look of the fey enchantress, startling to the point of dazzling and ever so slightly ethereal—the kiss of a sheer raspberry blush upon the apple of the cheeks, a slick of iridescent gloss to cherry red lips, and candy-floss eyes ranging from the azure blues and glistening emerald greens of the ocean to chalky violet blossom, all sparkly glitter and blended to perfection, and don't forget to play up your cheekbones and cupid's bow with dabs of shining highlighter.

The eyes are the windows to the soul, so start by accentuating the color and shape. To make blue peepers pop, choose shimmering pinks. Gray-green beauties work well with voluptuous violet shades swept along the eyelid. Brown eyes suit aquamarine and silvery blue hues, but really, there are no rules. If you were a fairy queen, you wouldn't follow the crowd. You'd develop your own spellbinding style.

Not sure where to start? Have fun playing with color, shimmer, and sparkle, and your magical look will emerge.

"When I look in the mirror, I see a unicorn, a fabulous, gorgeous unicorn."

unicorn nails

You've nailed the face, now nail the nails.

Uni-nails are the big thing in fashion and beauty. Whether you go for delicate pastels with a supersheen and filed to a point, or bold acrylics and rainbow brights, there's a plethora of styles to choose from—and since it's nail art, you don't have to commit. Simply change it to suit your mood or outfit.

RAINBOW NAIL ART

Create playful rainbows on alternate or accent nails like in the example here. Simply mask off areas of your nail by sticking on strips of craft tape, moving down the nail as you paint, waiting for each color to dry before moving on.

Feeling light and airy? Go for an ethereal gleam with drops of pale moonstone-colored polish. Want to make a magical statement? Luscious blueberry with a juicy sparkle should do it. For full-on unicorn boys and girls, how about sporting a hand of bright nails, resplendently iridescent and all the colors of the rainbow?

It's best to visit an experienced nail technician for some of the fancier styles, but there is a way to achieve the unicorn look that you can try at home. Go for a simple design that you can manage on your own nails.

GLITTER NAILS

For an easy but magical look, paint your nails in a bright fuchsia, then brush on holographic glitter nail polish onto the ends of your nails.

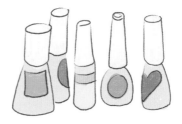

enchanting scents

It doesn't stop with the way you look. To take unicorn magic to heart you really need to feel it on the inside. Bring out your innate beauty by introducing a touch of unicorn to your cleansing rituals. Make pampering and preening an opportunity to bring fey sparkle into your life, and you'll feel unicorn every day.

Bath confetti

It comes in all shapes and sizes, from tiny rosebud petals to gold and silver glitter, and it smells heavenly. Add a sprinkle to your bath, immerse yourself in the bubbles, and breathe deeply!

Bath bombs

Pick gorgeous marshmallow shades and scents that remind you of spring blossom, then let them work their magic, with a slow-burning fizzle.

Oils

Experiment with essential oils. Go for natural scents that make you think of glorious meadows and rainbow-filled skies, things like rose, lavender, ylang ylang, and geranium. Add two or three drops to your bath water and inhale. Bliss!

Glistening body butters and lotions

They do exist and, just like unicorns, they'll add a touch of sparkle to your life. Choose soft scents and massage into the skin morning and night for a healthy iridescent glow.

how to wear it unicorn-style

You may have the hair, the make-up, and the nails, but there's something else you need to truly unleash your magical side—some unicorn sass. These mythical maestros may appear to be shy and retiring, but in all truth, they're 100% comfortable and confident in their own resplendent skin. They don't have to impress. They don't have to take center stage, unless they want to. They simply are, there in the moment, exuding a purity and grace that is captivating to behold.

There's something childlike about their aura, an innocence that is both delicate and playful. They're not afraid to have fun, to be different, to do their own unicorn thing. Most importantly they recognize that magic is everywhere, in every corner of the world, in every heartbeat, in the changing of the seasons, and the fleeting smile of a stranger. This is what makes them seem to light up from the inside.

While you pay homage to this glorious creature in whatever way you choose, remember to love yourself. Acknowledge all the wonderful things you've got going on, and be happy being you. When you do this, you truly wear it unicorn-style!

PART 4

UNICORN
Eats

what is a unicorn's favorite food?

They may be mythical beings, but surely they eat? It's easy to think they live on fresh air or, more fittingly, sunshine, rainbows, and love, but in reality, if one were to exist, it would have to feed. So, what would be its food of choice?

The common theory is that unicorns, like horses, prefer oats, hay, and grass. After all, they're so closely related it makes sense that their diets would follow suit. Natural herbivores, they'd also be drawn to flowers and plants that grow near water. A few schools of thought suggest that unicorns could be carnivores—they do have a giant horn protruding from their forehead, which would make an excellent weapon—but this is generally believed to be nonsense. Most unicorn lovers agree, these playful creatures couldn't harm another living thing.

Add some color to frosting with a couple of drops of food coloring of your choice.

Their endearing nature suggests a sweet tooth and a liking for things that look delightful, too. With this in mind, here is a list of foods that unicorns would probably like to see on the menu, should they make a surprise visit to your home.

* **Cake:** Cake, and more cake, smothered in pretty frosting.
* **Ice cream:** Think strawberry, raspberry, blueberry, in fact any berry, and of course vanilla, all liberally decorated with flavored sauces and mountains of sprinkles.
* **Candy:** Doesn't matter which type or brand, just anything rainbow-colored.
* **Pancakes:** Covered in sticky syrup and adorned with horn-like swirls of cream and sprinkles.
* **Unicorn toast:** See recipe suggestion on page 118.
* **Cookies:** Although they like any kind of sugary snack, cookies are their favorite, particularly coated with a layer of confectioner's/icing sugar.
* **Bananas:** Preferably covered in sticky toffee sauce. The shape is a nod to their horn, and it's one of their five a day!
* **Cotton candy:** It's light and ethereal, just like they are.
* **Multicolored jello in a unicorn-shaped mold:** They know that imitation is the biggest form of flattery.
* **Rainbow-colored salads, pastas, and other savory dishes:** Unicorns have a lot of energy and eat their vegetables!
* **Mashed potato:** This is an odd one, but they do love anything light and fluffy. Add a swirl of beetroot juice for subtle sweetness and a raspberry-ripple effect.

AND TO DRINK?

* **Water** obviously. They love the stuff, but it has to be fresh from a stream or river.
* **Milkshake** made with cream and ice cream in a selection of rainbow shades.
* **Cocoa** They're partial to a nicely presented cup of hot chocolate, with marshmallows and sparkles.
* **Unicorn cocktails** They do like a pretty cocktail or mocktail, especially if it's made in their honor and exquisitely decorated. It appeals to their sense of fun.

Now you know their favorite eats and drinks, you can practice getting it just right by having a go at some of the following recipes. Whether you've a sweet tooth or you like to be superhealthy, you can adapt what you make to suit your taste and budget.

TREATS & SNACKS

What could be more adorable than unicorn cakes, cookies, and cupcakes? They're sweet, petite, and sumptuously pretty. They make the perfect gift, whether you want to show you care or simply indulge yourself. Try the unicorn cupcakes—they represent pleasure in a small but delicately formed package. What's more, you don't have to be a star baker to have a go. There are also colorful breakfasts and savory snacks that capture the fun at the heart of unicorns. You can have unicorn-inspired treats for every meal!

UNICORN CUPCAKES

½ cup/115 g superfine/
caster sugar

¼ teaspoon dried
lavender flowers

1 stick/115 g unsalted
butter, at room
temperature

2 eggs

1 cup/115 g self-rising
flour

2 tablespoons milk

frosting:

1½ cups/220 g
confectioners'/icing sugar

1 stick/115 g butter,
at room temperature

1 teaspoon vanilla extract

1 tablespoon milk

sprinkles of your choice

**ready-made sugar ears,
flowers, and horn
(optional)**

a 12-hole cupcake pan/tin,
lined with paper cases

a piping bag, fitted with a
large star tip/nozzle

MAKES 12 CAKES

Subtly scented with lavender, these cupcakes are super simple to make, so go wild with decorations!

Preheat the oven to 350°F (180°C) Gas 4.

Put the sugar and lavender flowers in a food processor and process briefly to combine. Tip the lavender sugar into a bowl with the butter and beat together until pale and fluffy.

Beat the eggs into the butter mixture, one at a time, then sift in the flour and fold in. Stir in the milk.

Spoon the mixture into the paper cases. Bake in the preheated oven for about 18 minutes until risen and golden and a skewer inserted in the center comes out clean. Transfer to a wire rack to cool.

To make the frosting, sift the confectioners'/icing sugar into a mixing bowl and add the butter, vanilla extract, and milk. Beat together until you have a thick frosting. Spoon the frosting into the piping bag and pipe a generous swirl of frosting onto each cake. To finish, add some sprinkles and the sugar ears, flowers, and horn, if using.

CRANBERRY AND WHITE CHOCOLATE CUPCAKES

Bursting with cranberries and white chocolate and topped with a pretty pastel-colored swirled buttermilk frosting—these are perfect for a unicorn party!

YOU WILL NEED

1/2 stick/60 g butter, at room temperature

1/3 cup/60 g superfine/ caster sugar

1 egg

1/2 cup/60 g self-rising flour plus 1 teaspoon baking powder

1/3 cup/30 g pecans, finely ground

1/2 cup/60 g dried cranberries

1/3 cup/50 g white chocolate chips

2 tablespoons buttermilk

frosting:

1 1/2 cups/220 g confectioners'/ icing sugar

1 stick/115 g butter, at room temperature

1 teaspoon vanilla extract

1 tablespoon buttermilk

pink food coloring

sprinkles of your choice

a 12-hole cupcake pan/tin, lined with paper cases

a piping bag, fitted with a large star tip/nozzle

MAKES 12 CAKES

Preheat the oven to 350°F (180°C) Gas 4.

Put the butter and sugar in a mixing bowl and whisk until light and creamy. Add the egg and whisk again. Fold in the flour, baking powder, ground pecans, cranberries, chocolate chips, and buttermilk using a spatula or large spoon. Divide the batter between the paper cases. Bake in the preheated oven for 15–20 minutes, until the cakes are golden brown and spring back to the touch. Transfer to a wire rack to cool.

To make the frosting, sift the confectioners'/icing sugar into a mixing bowl and add the butter, vanilla extract, and buttermilk. Beat together until you have a thick frosting. Put half the frosting in a separate bowl and mix in a few drops of pink food coloring. Spoon the frosting into the piping bag, spreading the pink one along one side of the bag and the uncolored cream one along the other side, so that when you squeeze it the frosting is striped. Pipe a generous swirl of frosting onto each cake, add some sprinkles, and dust with confectioners'/icing sugar.

OMBRÉ LAYER CAKE

There's nothing more impressive than a magnificently constructed cake with many layers, and this spectacular cake with a delicate pink color palette and pistachio cream will wow your guests. For extra sparkle, add glitter or rose petals, or whatever takes your fancy. This is perfect for a special friend's birthday.

YOU WILL NEED

3 sticks/340 g butter, softened

1¾ cups/340 g superfine/caster sugar

6 eggs

2½ cups/340 g self-rising flour, sifted

3 teaspoons baking powder

3 tablespoons buttermilk or sour cream

3 teaspoons pure vanilla extract

pink food coloring gel

for the pistachio cream:

1⅓ cups/200 g shelled pistachio nuts

2 heaped tablespoons confectioners'/icing sugar

2⅓ cups/600 ml heavy/double cream

5 x 8-inch/20-cm round cake pans, greased and lined with baking parchment

a piping bag fitted with round tip/nozzle

SERVES 12

Use an electric whisk to mix the butter and sugar in a bowl until light and creamy. Add the eggs and whisk again. Fold in the flour, baking powder, and buttermilk or sour cream using a spatula, until incorporated.

To prepare the pistachio cream, blitz three-quarters of the pistachios in a food processor with the confectioners'/icing sugar to very fine crumbs. Set aside until you are ready to assemble the cake. Coarsely chop the remaining pistachios, and set aside for the decoration.

Preheat the oven to 350°F (180°C) Gas 4.

Fold the vanilla extract into the cake batter and divide the mixture equally between 5 bowls. Add a little food coloring to each, adding a very small amount in the first bowl and then increasing gradually in each bowl so that you have gradating colors of cake batter. Spoon each batter into a prepared cake pan. (If you do not have 5 pans, then cook the cakes in batches, washing, greasing, and re-lining the cake pans between cooking.) Bake for 20–25 minutes, until the cakes spring back to the touch and a knife inserted into the center of each cake comes out clean. Let cool in the pans for a few minutes, then turn out onto a wire rack to cool completely.

If the sides of the cakes have browned slightly during cooking, once cool, use a sharp knife to trim the sides of the cake carefully to expose the pink color.

Put the heavy/double cream in a large bowl with the ground pistachio and confectioners'/icing sugar mixture, and whisk to stiff peaks with an electric mixer or whisk. Spoon the cream into the piping bag.

Place the darkest pink cake on a serving plate and pipe a thick swirl of cream on top, ensuring that the cream goes to the edge of the cake. Repeat with the remaining cakes, stacking them in color order from darkest to lightest. Once the final layer is in place, smooth the edges of the cream using a palette knife or metal spatula. Pipe a layer of cream on top and smooth it neatly using a palette knife or metal spatula, then gently press the chopped pistachios around the edge of the cream.

Serve straight away or store in the refrigerator until you are ready to serve. As the cake contains fresh cream, it is best eaten on the day it is made, although it will keep for up to 2 days in the refrigerator.

ICED GEMS

These magical little morsels are topped with crunchy swirls of colored icing—a decadent version of the cookies you may remember from your childhood.

YOU WILL NEED

1⅓ cups/180 g plain/all-purpose flour

⅔ cup/120 g superfine/caster sugar

1 stick/120 g butter

1 egg, separated

frosting:

2½ cups/320 g confectioners'/icing sugar

food coloring gels

a very small cookie cutter

2 baking sheets lined with baking parchment

2–3 piping bags with star tips/nozzles

MAKES OVER 100

Preheat the oven to 350°F (180°C) Gas 4.

Put the flour into a large mixing bowl and stir in the sugar. Rub in the butter until the mixture resembles fine breadcrumbs. Add the egg yolk and draw the mixture together to form a smooth, soft dough.

On a clean, lightly floured work surface, roll the dough out into a large rectangle with a thickness of about ¼ in/4 mm. Cut out tiny circles using the cookie cutter or the end of a piping tip/nozzle. Bring the trimmed dough together and roll out again to cut as many cookies out of the dough as possible. Arrange the circles on the prepared baking sheets.

Bake in the preheated oven for about 4 minutes, until golden and firm.

Let cool on the baking sheet.

Meanwhile, whisk the egg white until light and add the confectioners'/icing sugar. Mix until very thick and smooth. Divide the mixture into two or three batches and color each with a little coloring gel.

Spoon the icing into the piping bags and pipe a rosette on the top of each cookie. Let dry for a couple of hours before serving or store in an airtight container or cookie jar and eat within 3 days.

MERINGUE SUGAR CLOUDS

Crisp on the outside and chewy in the middle, meringues are so fun! Their sweet simplicity of flavor combines particularly well with fresh fruit. Make them into nests and top with whipped cream and berries for a lovely dessert, or sandwich shells together for a teatime treat.

YOU WILL NEED

3 egg whites

½ teaspoon white vinegar

¼ teaspoon vanilla extract

1 cup/180g superfine/caster sugar

to serve:

2½ cups/600 ml whipping cream

3 tablespoons superfine/caster sugar

fresh fruit of your choice

2 baking sheets lined with non-stick baking parchment

MAKES ABOUT 20

Preheat oven to 225°F (110°C) Gas ¼.

Put the egg whites, vinegar, and vanilla into a large, clean, grease-free bowl and whisk on high speed with an electric hand whisk until it has doubled in volume and stiff peaks are formed. Add about a third of the sugar and beat on high speed for 5 minutes until all the sugar is dissolved. Repeat this process, adding the sugar a third at a time and beating for 5 minutes between each addition. The mixture should become stiff.

Scoop spoonfuls of the mixture onto the prepared baking sheets to form mounds of the desired size. Make a dip in each

one with the spoon to form a nest shape.

Bake the meringues in the preheated oven for about 60–80 minutes, or until they sound crispy and hollow when tapped underneath. Turn off the oven and leave them to cool in the oven with the door ajar for about 30 minutes. Remove from the oven and transfer to a wire rack to cool completely.

To serve, whip the cream and sugar with an electric hand whisk until soft peaks are formed. Serve the meringue nests topped with whipped cream and fresh fruit of your choice.

The meringues will keep for 14 days in an airtight container, or can be frozen for up to 2 months.

YOU WILL NEED

160 g/1¼ cups self-rising flour, sifted

1 teaspoon baking powder

1 egg, separated

1 teaspoon vanilla extract

scant ⅓ cup/60 g superfine/caster sugar

a pinch of salt

1 cup/250 ml milk

3 tablespoons melted butter, plus extra for frying

sprinkles, berries, and maple syrup, to decorate

a large skillet/frying pan or griddle

MAKES 12

UNICORN PANCAKES

For a light and fluffy breakfast, you can't go far wrong with sweet pancakes. Ideal as a birthday brunch, or a romantic treat, but they are so good you could have them anytime you needed a pick-me-up.

To make the pancake batter, put the flour, baking powder, egg yolk, vanilla extract, superfine/caster sugar, salt, and milk in a large mixing bowl and whisk together. Add in the melted butter and whisk again. The batter should have a smooth, dropping consistency.

In a separate bowl, whisk the egg white to stiff peaks. Gently fold the whisked egg white into the batter mixture using a spatula. Cover and put in the refrigerator to rest for 30 minutes.

When you are ready to serve, remove your batter mixture from the refrigerator and stir once. Put a little butter in a large skillet/frying pan set over medium heat. Allow the butter to melt and coat the base of the pan, then ladle small amounts of the rested batter into the pan, leaving a little space between each, or if you want to make larger pancakes you can fill the pan to make one at a time. Cook until the underside of each pancake is golden brown and a few bubbles start to appear on the top—this will take about 2–3 minutes. Turn the pancakes over using a spatula and cook on the other side until golden brown. Cook the remaining batter in the same way in batches until it is all used up, adding a little butter to the pan each time, if required.

Serve the pancakes in a stack with your choice of sprinkles or berries, and a drizzle of maple syrup on top.

UNICORN TOAST

Any self-respecting unicorn fan would be proud to munch on this delightful snack. Unleash your creativity by playing with color schemes, and don't forget the sprinkles!

YOU WILL NEED

a couple of slices of freshly made toast

a large tub of cream cheese or, if you prefer, natural or coconut yogurt

for the colors:

pink: beet or pomegranate juice

yellow: turmeric paste

purple: blueberry juice

green: matcha or spirulina powder

MAKES 2 slices

Use a separate pot for each color. Add two or three tablespoons of cream cheese or yogurt and then mix in your color dye. Start by adding a couple of drops, and increase the amount if you're going for a deeper, more intense shade.

Think of your toast as a blank canvas. Smear each slice with a thin base of plain cream cheese or yogurt.

Next, consider your palette. Smear on the colors of your choice, making sure you cover the surface, and swirl them around with the knife to create a unique pattern.

If you like, accessorize with your choice of sprinkles and then sit back and delight at your artistry, before eating!

RAINBOW BIRCHER MUESLI

If you're looking for a hearty and bewitching breakfast, something to revitalize your energy and help you canter through the day with renewed zest, it has to be this colorful and delicious Bircher muesli. It combines heart healthy oats with fragrant fruit to create a summer daydream.

YOU WILL NEED

1 cup/125 g rolled oats

½ cup/75 g (golden) raisins

¾ cup/175 ml apple juice

freshly squeezed juice of 1 lemon

¼ cup/100 g plain yogurt

1 apple, cored, peeled, and grated

3 tablespoons slivered/ flaked almonds

mixed summer fruit, to serve

clear honey, to serve

SERVES 4–6

Put the oats and raisins in a large dish. Pour over the apple and lemon juices. Cover with a dish cloth and let soak overnight. Alternatively, place in an airtight container and refrigerate, especially if the weather is hot.

The next morning when you're ready for breakfast, stir the yogurt, apple, and almonds into the soaked muesli. Divide between 4–6 bowls, arrange some brightly colored fruit over the top in a rainbow pattern and finish with a zigzag of honey.

SHOOTS AND FLOWERS

Edible flowers, as well as being beautiful, naturally lend themselves to salads, adding both color and flavor (and magic!). Here, zucchini/courgette, nasturtium, and chive flowers are used, but feel free to experiment with others such as borage, marigolds, violas, and pansies. Do make sure that the flowers have been grown organically and check that they are edible before use.

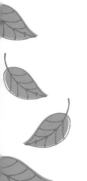

YOU WILL NEED

2 tablespoons extra virgin olive oil, plus extra for drizzling

1 yellow zucchini/courgette, sliced diagonally, plus flower, halved, if available

1 green zucchini/courgette, sliced diagonally, plus flower, halved, if available

3³/₄ oz/100 g arugula/rocket leaves

6 oz/180 g char-grilled artichokes

a handful of small nasturtium flowers

10 chive stems, snipped (with flowers if possible)

1 tablespoon lemon thyme leaves

freshly squeezed juice of ¹/₂ lemon

8 nasturtium flowers

sea salt and freshly ground black pepper

SERVES 4

Heat the olive oil in a large skillet/frying pan over a medium heat and sauté the sliced zucchini/courgettes for 5 minutes, turning once, until tender and slightly golden. Let cool slightly.

Put the arugula/rocket on a serving plate and top with the zucchini/courgettes, artichokes, nasturtium leaves, snipped chives, and lemon thyme. Squeeze over the lemon juice and drizzle with a little extra olive oil. Season and toss gently until combined.

Just before serving, garnish with the flowers.

UNICORN DRINKS

Food is not the only thing to be given the fey twist. Drinks can also be sprinkled with enchantment and served with flair. Unicorn cocktails and hot drinks are made with a combination of specially selected sweet and fruity ingredients, but even more important than the taste is how they are presented. The secret is to imagine you're dressing a shop window. Think elaborate and give each cocktail special attention. Practice your recipe so that you get the perfect colors and decorations. This is not something you throw together like a punch. This is exquisite, alluring, and far too pretty for words!

Before you commence your mythical mixing, invest in a few essentials.

* Different shaped glasses are a must, particularly long slender horn-shaped ones for obvious reasons.
* Edible glitter in every shade. This can be used to decorate the drink and also the rim of the glass.
* Pretty cocktail stirrers are a great investment. Go for rainbow-colored swirls and pastel shades.
* Edible flowers for decoration.
* Unicorn-shaped ice-cube molds.

There's an array of recipes to try, but any cocktail can be given the unicorn treatment. Experiment to find one that suits your taste and then think of ways to introduce color and sparkle. Here are a few top suggestions to get you started. Again, the ingredients can be changed, and the alcohol substituted with fruit juices and colorings.

YOU WILL NEED

1 lime, cut into 6 wedges

5 small blackcurrant leaves, 3 whole and 2 finely sliced

1 teaspoon demerara/ turbinado sugar

¾ oz (22 ml) Wild Hibiscus Syrup (see below right)

2 oz (60 ml) spiced rum

Soda water

to garnish:

sprig of blackcurrant sage in flower, blackcurrant leaves, and hollyhock flower

muddler, stirring rod

Collins glass

ice cubes

SERVES 1

HIBISCUS AND BLACKCURRANT LEAF MOJITO

The beautiful flowers of blackcurrant sage (*Salvia microphylla*) and blackcurrant leaves in the mid-summer provide the inspiration for this cocktail. As well as being very dramatic, the hibiscus syrup is very high in vitamin C.

For the Wild Hibiscus Syrup, add equal volumes of dried hibiscus flowers, sugar, and water—for example, 1 cup of flowers, 1 cup of superfine/caster sugar, and 1 cup of water—to a non-reactive pan

and bring to a boil.
Remove from the heat
and let the ingredients
steep for 20 minutes.
Strain, reserving the
flower as a garnish.

Put 4 wedges of lime,
3 whole blackcurrant
leaves, and the sugar
in the glass, and
muddle. Add the Wild
Hibiscus Syrup. Half-fill
the glass with ice. Add
the rum, the remaining
2 lime wedges, and
the 2 finely sliced
blackcurrant leaves.
Top with soda water
and serve with a
stirring rod (straw or
spoon if not!). Garnish
with the sprig of
blackcurrant sage
flowers and
blackcurrant leaves.
You could add a
hollyhock flower, too.

2 oz (60 ml) Lavender Gin

³/₄ oz (22 ml) Honey Syrup
(see below right)

³/₄ oz (22 ml) freshly
squeezed lemon juice

dash of Parfait Amour

dash of orange bitters

soda water

lavender sprig, to garnish

cocktail shaker with strainer

Collins glass

ice cubes

straw

SERVES 1

LAVENDER GIN FIZZ

Lavender is a favorite flower of unicorns. Here it combines particularly well with honey, citrus, and bitter flavors. Adding a dash of Parfait Amour (a dark purple liqueur, flavored with rose and violet petals, vanilla beans/pods, and orange blossom) intensifies the lavender color.

For the honey syrup, simply combine equal parts honey and water, and heat until the honey is thoroughly dissolved to give a delicious simple floral syrup.

Fill the glass with ice. Add all the ingredients, except the soda water, to the cocktail shaker and fill it two-thirds full with ice. Cover and shake hard for 20 seconds. Strain the mixture into the chilled glass over the ice. Cut a sprig of lavender to fit just above the rim of the glass. Top with soda water. Add the straw and serve.

UNICORN MILKSHAKES

Milkshakes are a dessert in a glass. They can be healthy, or naughty, and they can also be unicorn. Again, when it comes to flavors and consistency, it's down to personal preference. Here are a couple of delicious recipes, which have been given the magical treatment. Simply adapt to suit your taste.

GOLDEN SUNSHINE MILKSHAKE

A sweet and tasty burst of pure joy, this milkshake has a crunchy candy topping for a fun surprise.

Put two scoops of the ice cream in a blender with the milk and three quarters of the chocolate-covered sponge candy/honeycomb, and blitz until thick and creamy.

Pour the milkshake into the chilled glasses, top each glass with a second scoop of ice cream, and sprinkle with the remaining chopped sponge candy/honeycomb.

Serve immediately with straws.

Tip: for extra sunshine, add some gold edible glitter on top!

YOU WILL NEED

4 scoops honeycomb or vanilla ice cream

2 cups/500 ml milk

1½ oz/40 g chocolate-covered sponge candy/honeycomb, roughly chopped

2 soda glasses, chilled

2 straws

SERVES 2

YOU WILL NEED

1²/₃ cups/400 ml milk, chilled

4 scoops rose ice cream (such as Kulfi) or vanilla ice cream

1–2 tablespoons rose syrup, to taste

3–4 fresh rose petals, thinly shredded, to decorate

rose Turkish delight, to serve (optional)

SERVES 4

ROSE PETAL DREAM

These milkshakes look as pretty as a picture in this pastel hue of pink. Serve with shredded rose petals on top for a fragrant, magical taste.

Put the milk and ice cream in a blender and blitz until frothy. Add the rose syrup to taste and blitz again. If you are using vanilla ice cream, add an extra spoonful of rose syrup for more rose flavor. Pour into chilled glasses and top with the shredded rose petals. Serve immediately with Turkish delight, if using.

EASY UNICORN COCOA

YOU WILL NEED

3½ oz/100 g milk chocolate, chopped

1 cup/250 ml milk

1 cup/250 ml heavy/ double cream

can of whipped cream

mini marshmallows, sprinkles, and edible glitter, to garnish

SERVES 2

What could be more satisfying than a cup of unicorn hot chocolate? It's creamy, sweet, and coated in loveliness, the perfect treat at the end of a long day or for those moments when you just want to drift off into daydream land. Even better, it's so simple to make you'll find you can't help sharing the magic!

Place the chopped chocolate in a heatproof bowl over a pan of simmering water and heat over low heat until melted. Spoon the melted chocolate into a saucepan with the milk and cream, and heat over low heat, whisking all the time. Pour the hot chocolate into glasses.

Squirt a swirl of whipped cream on top of the hot cocoa and decorate with mini marshmallows, sprinkles, and glitter.

Serve immediately.

the unicorn twist

Any type of meal can be given a unicorn twist. The idea is to be creative and playful with food. Think about the taste, of course, but also how the meal is put together and the picture it creates on the plate. We eat with our eyes, so make each meal a magical feast and you'll savor the experience.

* **Blend food colors as if you're putting together a piece of art:** Think soft muted greens blending into vibrant blue, by choosing salad leaves or greens that fuse together easily, pinks that merge into bright berry red, or orange and lemon shades. You don't have to combine every single food group in this way, but you can add touches of style by using prettily colored dips and sauces.

* **Edible flowers are perfect with salads and soups and add a glimmer of fairy-tale magic:** Think gorgeous meadows where unicorns frolic; then get picking and aim to recreate the vista.

* **Edible glitter is another way to give any meal some unicorn sparkle:** Sprinkle liberally, or have a go at creating a swirling pattern. Add to drinks, desserts, and breakfast cereals.

* **Plates and table accessories can have unicorn flair, too:** Choose rainbow-colored crockery, place mats, and napkins, or ones that have an iridescent sparkle. Think pink and gold, silver and turquoise, aquamarine and sky blue. The key is to experiment, putting colors together until you find something that says and feels "unicorn."
* **For fun, twist your napkins into the shape of a unicorn horn** and secure in place with a napkin ring.
* **Make your dining experience uniquely unicorn by creating an enchanting centerpiece for the table:** This could be in the shape of a unicorn horn, or a bowl that resembles a cornucopia filled with candy and other treats. You could even use a model or sculpture of a unicorn and surround it with fresh flowers. Let your imagination take the reins and be theatrical.

UNICORN TIP

Have some fun and throw your very own unicorn dinner party or masked ball. You have all the essential ingredients and know-how, from how to make delicious treats that look spectacular, to creating and sporting a stunning unicorn look for the event. What are you waiting for?

the unicorn creed

Foster an open and loving heart.
Be kind, to others and yourself.
Be hopeful and look for the silver lining.
Trust that everything is working out perfectly.
Shine your light at all times.
Adopt a playful spirit.
Be bold, step outside of your comfort zone,
and feel your world expand.
Don't be afraid to go your own way; you are
unique, so carve a path that works for you.
Be thankful for life's blessings.
Tread softly and with grace in all
your dealings.
Recognize the magic that is all around you.
And finally …
If in doubt,
In any situation,
Embrace your inner unicorn.

a final word

The unicorn is special.
It is sacred.
It transmits love and symbolizes purity.
It is free to roam, anywhere, at any time.
It captures hearts and releases them from
pain and pressure.
It provides hope and comfort and exudes
playful energy.
And it always lights the way.
All these things it does with a sprinkling of
sweetness and a loving heart.

The unicorn makes life that bit more magical.
It doesn't matter how you choose to
celebrate it, whether in verse, art, magic, or
with style and cooking finesse—
just have fun and spread the love!

Whether you realize it or not—
we are all a bit "unicorn."

index

recipe credits

Hannah Miles
Cranberry and white chocolate
cupcakes p.106–107
Ombre layer cake p.108–110
Golden sunshine milkshake
(adapted) p.131
Rose petal dream p.132
Easy unicorn cocoa (adapted) p.134

Julian Day
Meringue sugar clouds p.114–115

Liz Franklin
Ice gems p.112–113

Lottie Muir
Hibiscus and blackcurrant leaf
mojito p.126
Lavender gin fizz p.128

Nicola Graimes
Shoots and flowers p.122

Susannah Blake
Unicorn cupcakes (adapted) p.104

Tonia George
Rainbow bircher muesli
(adapted) p.120

photography credits

All images are listed and
credited where they first
appear in the book.

Kate Whitaker p.113, 131,
133, 137
Kim Lightbody p.124, 126,
127, 129
Laura Edwards p.134
Matt Russell p.123
Steve Painter p.111, 115, 116
William Reavell p.107

Getty Images:
istock:
/Azurita p.121
/Drogatnev p.56
/Duncan1890 p.73
/Eatsmarter_de p.119

/egal p.3
/FarmVeld p.102–103
(background)
/Kumer p.37
/malija p.6–7 (background)
/Mila_1989 p.53
/MichalLudwiczak p.91
/Nevarpp p.19
/NikkiZalewski p.52
/NYS444 p.2, 38
/Saneeya Bureekhan p.71
/SSpino p.59

EyeEm:
/Freddie Lindell p.23
/Liam Mcgrady p.50
/Michael Lyman p.58
/Nuno Filipe Pereira p.16

Archive Photos:
/D. Corson/ClassicStock p.45

Oxford Scientific:
/David Clapp p.46–47

Cultura:
/Eugenio Marongiu p.48

Photographer's Choice:
/Cathy Collins p.49
/Don Landwehrle p.51

UpperCut Images:
/Roy Hsu p.55

Moment:
/QuiLie p.95 (top right)